PIANO • VOCAL • GUITAR

BEST SONGS OF THE

2 American Pie
12 Baby What A Big Surprise
16 Baby, I'm-A Want You
26 Bohemian Rhapsody
36 Can't Smile Without You
40 (They Long To Be) Close To You
44 Copacabana (At The Copa)
54 Daniel
21 Dust In The Wind
58 Fire And Rain
51 For All We Know
62 How Can You Mend A Broken Heart
68 I Feel The Earth Move
65 I Will Survive
74 I Write The Songs
78 If
81 Imagine
86 It Never Rains (In Southern California)
90 It's Impossible (Somos Novios)
94 It's Too Late
96 Just The Way You Are
103 Let It Be
108 Maggie May
111 Mandy
114 Me And Bobby McGee
120 Midnight Train To Georgia
117 Nadia's Theme
126 Piano Man
136 Precious And Few
140 Speak Softly, Love (Love Theme)
131 Stayin' Alive
142 The Way We Were
148 You Make Lovin' Fun
145 You Needed Me
152 You've Got A Friend
157 Your Song

0-7935-4227-8

AMERICAN PIE

Words and Music by
DON McLEAN

MCA music publishing

Em
Am
Em
Am
But Feb-ru-ar-y made me shiv-er with ev-'ry pa-per I'd de-liv-er.
C
G/B
Am
C
D
Bad news on the door-step I could-n't take one more step I
G
D/F#
Em
Am7
D
can't re-mem-ber if I cried when I read a-bout his wid-owed bride,
G
D/F#
Em
C
D7
G
C
Some-thing touched me deep in-side the day the mu-sic died.

Moderately
G
G
C
G
D
So bye - bye, Miss A - mer - i - can Pie Drove my
Chev - y to the lev - ee but the lev - ee was dry. Them
good ole boys were drink - in' whis - key and rye Sing - in'
To Coda
Em
A7
this - 'll be the day that I die,

Em
D7
This - 'll be the day that I die.
G
Am
1. Did you write the book of love and do you
2.-4. See additional lyrics
C
Am
Em
have faith in God a - bove?
If the Bi - ble tells
D
G
D/F#
you so
Now do you be - lieve in

Em
Am7
C
rock and roll. Can mu - sic save your mor - tal soul and
Em
A7
D
can you teach me how to dance real slow?
Em
D
Well, I know that you're in love with him 'cause I
Em
D
C
G
saw you danc - in' in the gym, You both kicked off your shoes.

A7
C
D7
Man, I dig those rhy - thm and blues. I was a
G
D/F♯
Em
Am
lone - ly teen - age bronc - in' buck with a pink car - na - tion and a
C
G
D/F♯
Em
pick - up truck. But I knew I was out of luck the day
C
D7
G
C
the mu - sic died.

1,2,3
G
D7
4
G
D7
G
C
I start - ed sing - ing
He was sing - in' bye - bye, Miss A -
G
D
G
C
G
D
mer - i - can Pie Drove my Chev - y to the lev - ee but the lev - ee was dry.
Them
G
C
G
D
good ole boys were drink - in' whis - key and rye
Sing - in'
Em
A7
Em
this -'ll be the day that I die,
This -'ll be the day that I

D7
die.
rit.
Freely
G
D/F#
Em
Am
C
I met a girl who sang the blues and I asked her for some hap - py news, But
Em
D
she just smiled and turned a - way.
G
D/F#
Em
G
Am
G/B
C
I went down to the sa - cred store where I heard the mu - sic years be - fore But the

Em
C
D
man there said the mu - sic would - n't play.
And
Em
Am
Em
Am
in the streets the chil - dren screamed, the lov - ers cried and the po - ets dreamed. But
C
G/B
Am
C
D
G
D/F♯
Em
G/B
not a word was spo - ken the church bells all were bro-ken. And the three men I ad - mire most, the
C
D7
G
D/F♯
Em
Fa - ther, Son and the Ho - ly Ghost, They caught the last train for the coast the

Additional Lyrics

2. Now for ten years we've been on our own,
And moss grows fat on a rollin' stone
But that's not how it used to be
When the jester sang for the king and queen
In a coat he borrowed from James Dean
And a voice that came from you and me
Oh and while the king was looking down,
The jester stole his thorny crown
The courtroom was adjourned,
No verdict was returned
And while Lenin read a book on Marx
The quartet practiced in the park
And we sang dirges in the dark
The day the music died
We were singin'... bye-bye... etc.

3. Helter-skelter in the summer swelter
The birds flew off with a fallout shelter
Eight miles high and fallin' fast,
it landed foul on the grass
The players tried for a forward pass,
With the jester on the sidelines in a cast
Now the half-time air was sweet perfume
While the sergeants played a marching tune
We all got up to dance
But we never got the chance
'Cause the players tried to take the field,
The marching band refused to yield
Do you recall what was revealed
The day the music died
We started singin'... bye-bye... etc.

4. And there we were all in one place,
A generation lost in space
With no time left to start again
So come on, Jack be nimble, Jack be quick,
Jack Flash sat on a candlestick
'Cause fire is the devil's only friend
And as I watched him on the stage
My hands were clenched in fists of rage
No angel born in hell
Could break that Satan's spell
And as the flames climbed high into the night
To light the sacrificial rite
I saw Satan laughing with delight
The day the music died
He was singin'... bye-bye... etc.

BABY WHAT A BIG SURPRISE

Words and Music by
PETER CETERA

B♭
C
F
C/E
Dm7
Ba - by, what a big sur - prise; ___
B♭
C
F
1
E♭
3 fr
B♭
right be-fore my ver - y eyes, _ oh, oh, ___ oh, ___ oh.
2
C/E
E♭
3 fr
B♭
oh, ___ oh, ___ oh. ___
Am
G
C
Just to be ___ a - lone _ was a lit - tle more than I could take, ___

Am
G
C
then you came to stay.
Oo.
Am
G
Am
G/B
C
Hold me in the morn - ing, love me in the af - ter - noon.
Am
G
B♭
G/B
Help me find my way, hey, yeah.
C
Dm7
C7/E
F
C/E
Dm
Now and then just like be - fore
I think

C Dm7 C7/E Fsus F C/E Dm
__ a - bout the love I've thrown __ a - way, but now __
C Dm7 C7/E F C7/E
__ it __ does - n't mat - ter an - y - way.
B♭ C F C/E Dm7
Ba - by, what a big sur - prise; __
B♭ C F E♭ 3fr B♭
Repeat and Fade
right be-fore my ve - ry eyes, _ oh, oh, __ oh, __ oh.

BABY, I'M-A WANT YOU

Words and Music by
DAVID GATES

Db/Eb
Ab
4fr
can't live with-out your lov-in' and af-fec-tion,
Bbm/Ab
Abmaj7
giv-in' me di-rec-tion like a guid-ing light to help me through my dark-est ho-ur.
Db
Db/C
Bbm7
Late-ly, I'm a-pray-in' that you'll al-ways be a-stay-in' be-side me.
Db/Eb
Ab
4fr
no chord

Cm7
3fr
Eb/Db
3fr
Db
Used to be my life was just _ e-mo - tions pass - ing _ by, _
Cm7
3fr
Eb/Db
3fr
Db
Ab
4fr
feel-ing all the while and nev - er real - ly know-ing _ why. _
Bbm7
Ab6
3fr
Db
Bbm7
Db/Eb
Late-ly, I'm a-pray-in' that you'll al - ways be _ a-stay - in' _ be - side _

Ab
no chord
Cm7
me.
Used to be my life was just emotions
Eb/Db
Db
Cm7
passing by.
Then you came along and made me laugh and
Eb/Db
Db
F7/A
Bbm
Db/Eb
made me cry.
You taught me why.
Ab
Bbm/Ab
Baby, I'm a-want you
Baby, I'm a-need you.

A♭maj7
G♭maj7/A♭
4fr
Oh, it took _ so long to find _ you, ba - by, Ba -
A♭
4fr
B♭/A♭
- by, I'm a - want_ you.
Ba-by, I'm a-need you.
A♭
4fr
D♭/A♭
4fr
A♭
4fr
B♭m/A♭
A♭maj7
D♭/A♭
4fr
Repeat and Fade

DUST IN THE WIND

Words and Music by
KERRY LIVGREN

C
G/B
Am
All my dreams
All we do
slips a - way.
G
Dm7
Am
To Coda
pass be - fore my eyes, a cu - ri - os - i - ty.
crum - bles to the ground though we re - fuse to see.
All your mon - ey won't an - oth - er min - ute buy.
D/F♯
G
Am
Am/G
Dust in the wind.
Dust in the wind.
1
D/F♯
G
Am
G/B
All they are is dust in the wind.

2
D/F♯
G
Am
All we are is dust in the wind.
G/A
F/A
Oh
Am
G/A
F/A

C
Am
D.S. al Coda
G/B
CODA
D/F♯
G
Dust in the
Am
Am/G
D/F♯
G
wind.
(All we are is dust in the

Am
Am/G
D/F#
G
wind.)
All we are is dust in the wind.
(Dust in the
Am
Am/G
D/F#
G
wind.)
Ev - 'ry - thing is dust in the wind.
(Ev - 'ry - thing is dust in the
Am
wind.)
Am
Repeat and Fade

BOHEMIAN RHAPSODY

Words and Music by
FREDDIE MERCURY

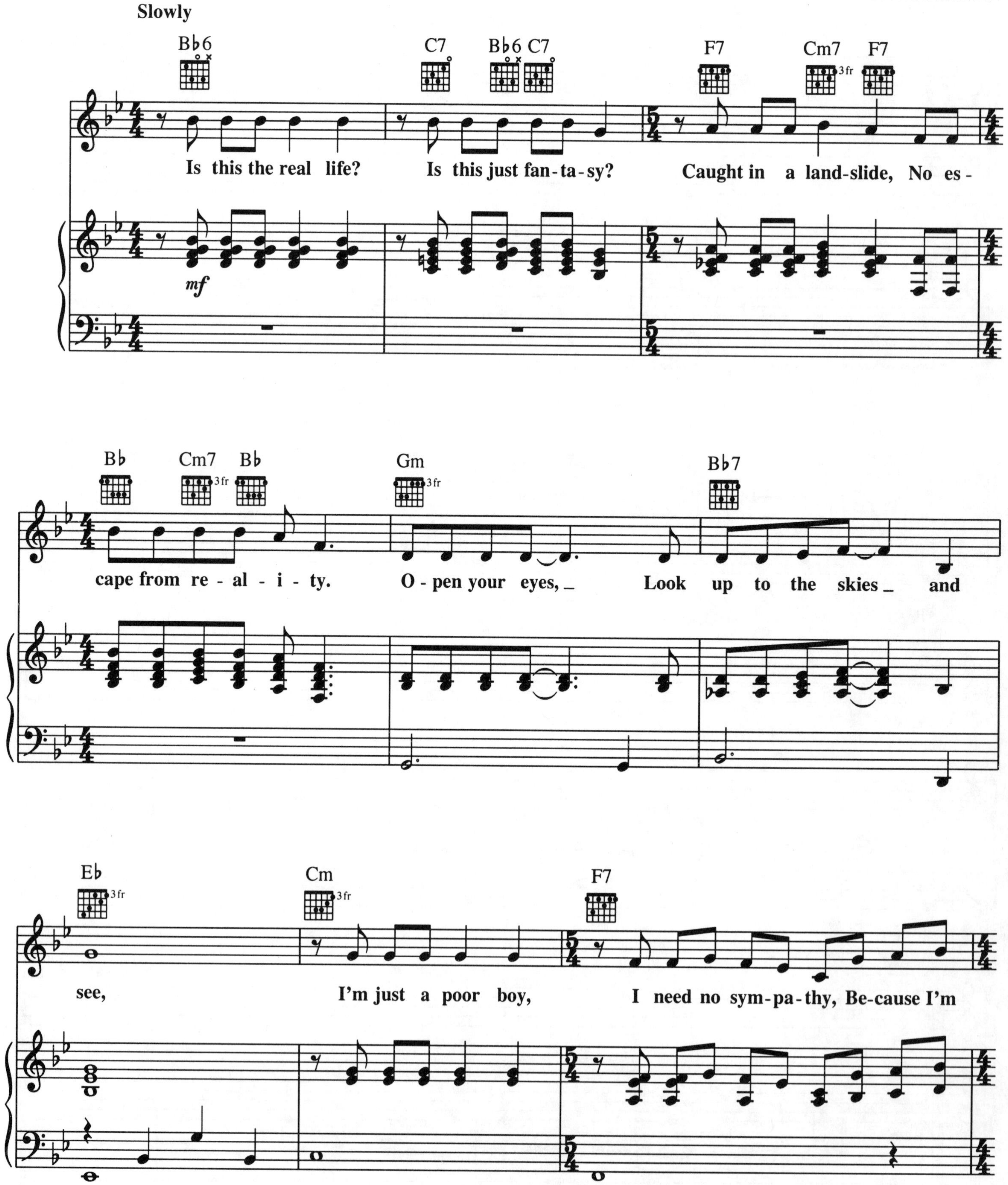
Slowly
Bb6
C7
Bb6 C7
F7
Cm7 3fr F7
Is this the real life? Is this just fan-ta-sy? Caught in a land-slide, No es-
mf
Bb
Cm7 3fr Bb
Gm 3fr
Bb7
cape from re-al-i-ty. O-pen your eyes, Look up to the skies and
Eb 3fr
Cm 3fr
F7
see, I'm just a poor boy, I need no sym-pa-thy, Be-cause I'm

B Bb A Bb B Bb A Bb Eb 3fr Bb/D
eas - y come, eas - y go, Lit - tle high, lit - tle low, An - y way the wind blows
C#dim7 F/C F Bb
does-n't real-ly mat - ter to me, to me.
Bb Gm 3fr Cm 3fr
Ma - ma just killed a man, Put a gun a-gainst his head, pulled my
Too late, my time has come, Sends shiv-ers down my spine, bod - y's
F Bb Gm 3fr
trig-ger, now he's dead. Ma - ma, life had just be-gun, But
ach-ing all the time. Good-bye, ev-'ry-bod - y I've got to go, Got-ta

Cm7
B+
E♭/B♭
F/A
Fm/A♭
E♭
B♭/D
3fr
6fr
now I've gone and thrown it all a - way.
leave you all be - hind and face the truth.
Ma - ma
ooh,
Ma - ma,
ooh,
Cm
Fm
B♭
Did-n't mean to make you cry.
If I'm not back a - gain this time to -
I don't want to die,
I some-times wish I'd nev-er been born at
1
E♭
B♭/D
Cm
A♭m
E♭
A♭/E♭
E♭
4fr
mor-row, car-ry on, car-ry on as if noth-ing real - ly mat - ters.
E♭dim
Fm7/E♭
B♭

2
E♭
B♭/D
Cm
Fm
all.
B♭7
E♭
Gm/D
Cm
Fm
D♭
D♭/C♭
B♭m
L'istesso tempo (♪ = ♩)
A
D/A
A
Adim
A
D/A
A
Adim
A
I see a lit - tle sil-hou - et - to of a man, Scar-a -

D/A A D/A A Adim A D/A A D♭/A♭ A♭
4fr 4fr
mouche, Scar - a-mouche, will you do the Fan - dan - go. Thun-der-bolt and light - ning,
Chorus:
f
C/G E A
no chord
ver - y, ver - y fright - 'ning me. (Gal - li - le - o.) Gal - li - le - o. (Gal - li - le - o.) Gal - li -
le - o, Gal - li - le - o fig - a - ro Mag - ni - fi - co.
(let ring - - - - - - - - - -)
B B♭ A B♭ B B♭ A B♭ A♭/E♭ E♭ E♭dim E♭
3fr 3fr
Solo: I'm just a poor boy and no - bod - y loves me. He's just a poor boy
Chorus:
mf
f

Ab/Eb Eb Ebdim Eb Ab Eb/G F Bb
3fr 3fr 4fr 3fr
from a poor fam - i - ly. Spare him his life from this mon - stros - i - ty.
mf
Ab Eb/G F#dim7 Fm7 B Bb A Bb B Bb A Bb
4fr 3fr
Solo: Eas - y come, eas - y go, will you let me go, Bis -
f
Eb Bb Eb Bb
3fr 3fr
Chorus:
mil - lah! No, we will not let you go. (Let him go!) Bis - mil - lah! We
Eb Bb
3fr
will not let you go. (Let him go!) Bis - mil - lah! We will not let you go. (Let me go.)

Gb7
Will not let you go. (Let me go) Will not let you go. (Let me go.) Ah.
Bm
A
D
Db
Gb
Bb
Eb
3fr
no chord
Eb
3fr
Solo:
No, no, no, no, no, no, no. (Oh ma-ma mi-a, ma-ma mi-a.) Ma-ma
Bb
Eb
3fr
Ab
4fr
D
Gm
3fr
mi-a, let me go. Be-el-ze-bub has a dev-il put a-side for
Bb
me, for me, for me.

Eb
3fr
F7
Bb7
Eb/Bb
6fr
So you think you can
Bb
Eb
3fr
Bb
Db
stone me and spit in my eye.
Bb7
Eb/Bb
6fr
Bb
Eb
3fr
Ab
4fr
So you think you can love me and leave me to die.

Fm
Bb
Fm
Oh, ___ ba - by, ___ can't do this to me,
Bb
Fm7
Bb
Fm7
Bb
ba - by, ___ Just got-ta get out, just got-ta get right out - ta
Eb
Bb7
here. _
poco a poco rit. e dim.
Slowly, a tempo
Eb
Bb/D
Cm
G/B
Cm
G7/B
Cm
Bb7
Eb
D
Gm
mf

Ab
Eb
Cm
Gm
Cm
Gm
Noth - ing real - ly mat - ters,
An - y - one can see,
Cm
Abm
Bb11
Eb
Ab/Eb
Noth - ing real - ly mat - ters,
Noth - ing real - ly mat - ters to me.
rit.
a tempo
Eb
Ebdim7
Bb/D
Bbm/Db
C7
C7b9
C7
F
Bb
F/A
Abdim7
Gm7
F
An - y way the wind blows.
poco a poco rit. e dim.
p

CAN'T SMILE WITHOUT YOU

Words and Music by CHRIS ARNOLD, DAVID MARTIN and GEOFF MORROW

Am
C/D
you on-ly knew what I'm go-ing through; I just can't smile with-out
G
C/D
G(add 9)
G
Em7
you. You came a-long just like a song and
Am7
C/D
D7
G(add 9)
G
Em7
bright-ened my day. Who'd-a be-lieved that you were part of a dream. Now it all seems
Am7
D7
C/E
D7/F#
G
light-years a-way. And now you know I Can't Smile With-out You.
Em
Am
I Can't Smile With-out You. I can't laugh and I can't sing I'm

C/D
D♭/E♭
A♭
find-ing it hard to do an-y-thing. You see, I feel sad when you're sad.
cresc.
mf
Fm
B♭m
I feel glad when you're glad. If you on-ly knew what I'm go-ing through;
3
D♭/E♭
E♭m7
I just can't smile. Now, some peo-ple say hap-pi-ness takes
A♭7
D♭maj7
D♭m
so ver-y long to find. Well, I'm find-ing it hard leav-ing your love be-hind
E♭7sus
E7sus
A
me. And you see, I Can't Smile With-out You.
f

F♯m
Bm
I Can't Smile With - out You. I can't laugh and I can't sing. I'm
D/E
E♭/F
B♭
find- ing it hard to do an - y - thing. You see, I feel glad when you.
cresc.
ff
you're glad. I feel sad when you're sad. If you on- ly knew what
Gm
Cm
Instrumental till fade
I'm go-ing through; I just can't smile with- out
Repeat and Fade

(THEY LONG TO BE)
CLOSE TO YOU

Words by HAL DAVID
Music by BURT BACHARACH

Abmaj7
G7sus
G7
Gm7
stars fall down from the sky ev-'ry time you walk
mp
Cm7
Ab
4fr
by? Just like me___ they long to be
mf
Eb6
Ebmaj7
Eb6
Ebmaj7
Ab
4fr
Ab6
Abmaj7
Ab6
close to you.___ On the day that you were born the
f

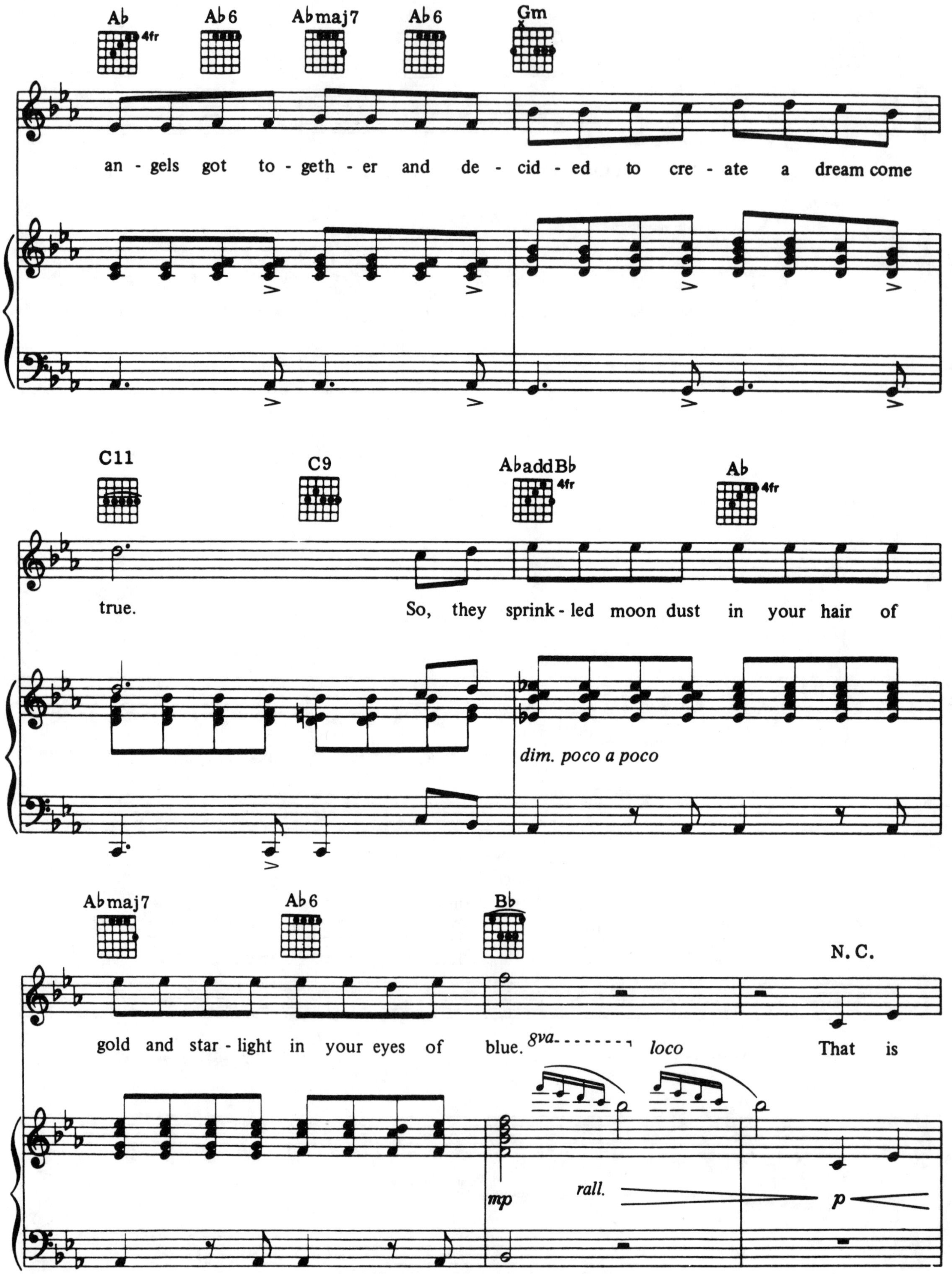
Ab
4fr
Ab6
Abmaj7
Ab6
Gm
an - gels got to - geth - er and de - cid - ed to cre - ate a dream come
C11
C9
AbaddBb
4fr
Ab
4fr
true. So, they sprink - led moon dust in your hair of
dim. poco a poco
Abmaj7
Ab6
Bb
N. C.
gold and star - light in your eyes of blue.
8va
loco
That is
mp
rall.
p

Abmaj7
G7sus
G7
Gm7
why all the {boys / girls} in town fol-low you all a-
mp a tempo
Cm7
Ab
4fr
round. Just like me__ they long to be
Eb6
Ebmaj7
Eb6
Ebmaj7
Ab
AbaddBb
close to you.__ Just like me__
dim. poco a poco
Ab
AbaddBb
Eb6
Ebmaj7
Eb6
Ebmaj7
they long to be close to you.__
keep repeating & fade out

COPACABANA
(AT THE COPA)

Words by BRUCE SUSSMAN and JACK FELDMAN
Music by BARRY MANILOW

Fm7 Bb11 Ebmaj7 Am7-5 D7
en - gue — and do the Cha - Cha, — And while she tried to be a star, To - ny
fin - ished, — he called her o - ver. — But Ri - co went a bit too far, To - ny
Dis - co, — but not for Lo - la. — Still in the dress she used to wear, fad - ed
Gm7 Cdim Gm
al - ways tend - ed bar, a - cross the crowd - ed — floor. They worked from
sailed a - cross the bar. And then the punch - es — flew and chairs were
feath - ers in her hair, She sits there so re - fined and drinks her -
Cdim D7-9 Gm Cm7 D7
eight to — four. They were young and they had each oth - er, who could
smashed in — two. There was blood and a sin - gle gun - shot, but just
self half — blind. She lost her youth and she lost her To - ny, now she's

Gm
D7 (F♯bass)
B♭7 (F bass)
Fm7
B♭11
E♭maj7
ask for more? who shot who? lost her mind! At the Co - pa, Co - pa - ca - ba - na, The
f
Fm7
B♭11
E♭maj7
C11
C7
Fm7
B♭11
hot - test spot north of Ha - va - na. At the Co - pa, Co - pa - ca
C11
C7
Fm7
B♭7
Gm7
C9
ba - na, mu - sic and pas - sion were al - ways the fash - ion, At the
Fm7
D7-9
Gm9
F♯m9
To Coda
Co - pa
they fell in love.
she lost her love.
Love,
mf

Fm9
F♯m9
Gm9
F♯m9
1.
Fm9
F♯m9
Gm9
Co - pa - ca - ba - na.
2. His name was
2. Fm9
F♯m9
Interlude:
Gm9
A♭m9
4 fr.
Am9
5fr
Co - pa,
Co - pa - ca -
poco a poco cresc.
B♭m9
6 fr.
Bm9
7 fr.
Cm9
8fr
D♭m9
9fr
ba - na,
Co - pa - ca - ba - na,
f
Ah,

Dm9
10fr
Ah,
Ah,
Ah.
Dm
Ah.
Eb
(Db bass)
Co - pa,
Co - pa - ca -

Fm (D bass)
ba - na, like in Ha - va - na,
have a ba - na - na, mu - sic and
Em
Ebm
Bbm9
6 fr.
Am9
5fr
Abm9
4 fr.
Gm9
Gbm9
pas - sion al - ways in fash - ion.
Fm9
No chord
Fm9
F#m9 Gm9
F#m9
mf
mf Instrumental Solo

Fm9
F#m9
Gm9
Abm9
4 fr
Am9
5fr
Abm9
4 fr.
Gm9
F#m9
Fm9
F#m9
Gm9
D. S. al Coda
Her name is
Coda
D7-9
Gm9
F#m9
Fm9
F#m9
Co - pa, —
don't — fall in love,
Co - pa - ca -
don't fall in
mf
Gm9
F#m9
Fm9
F#m9
Gm9
ba - na, —
love.
Co - pa - ca - ba - na. —
f

FOR ALL WE KNOW

from the Motion Picture LOVERS AND OTHER STRANGERS

Words by ROBB WILSON and JAMES GRIFFIN
Music by FRED KARLIN

Moderato, with a light beat

G A9 A7

Love, look at the two of us, Stran -

C6 Am Cm G Bm7

gers in man - y ways.

Em
G
A7
We've got a life - time to share. So much to
Dmaj7
Gmaj7
Cmaj7
D7sus
say And as we go from day to
G
A9
A7
day, I'll feel you close to me, But
two of us Stran -
C6
Cm
G
Bm7
time a - lone will tell.
gers in man - y ways.
Em
G
A7
Let's take a life - time to say, "I knew you

Dmaj7
Gmaj7
Cmaj7
well," For only time will tell us so
Bm7
Em
Em7
Cmaj7
D7sus
D9
And love may grow for all
G
D/G
C/G
D7/G
we know.
G
Gmaj7
C/G
D7
To Coda
G
(Waa)
Love
D.S. al Coda
Look at the
CODA
G
rit.

DANIEL

Words and Music by ELTON JOHN
and BERNIE TAUPIN

E7
Am
F
heading for Spain
Oh and
I can see Daniel waving good bye
ever seen
Oh and
he should know
he's been there enough
G
Am
God it looks like Daniel
Lord I miss Daniel
F
G7
F/G
To Coda
Must be the clouds in my eyes
Oh I miss him so much
1
C

2
C
F
Oh
Dan - iel my broth - er you are
C
F
old - er than me do you still feel the pain
Of the scars
C
Am
that won't heal your eyes have died
But you see more than I
F
Fm
C
A7
Dan - iel you're a star
In the face of the sky

Dm7
G7
D.S. twice
1st D.S. Instrumental ad lib. (small notes)
2nd D.S. 1st lyric again al Coda
CODA
C
Oh God it
F
looks like Dan - iel
G7
F/G
Must be the clouds in my eyes.
C
F
G
C
F
C

FIRE AND RAIN

Words and Music by
JAMES TAYLOR

C
Gm7
F
C
I walked out this morn - ing and I wrote down this song
My bod - y's ach - ing and my time is at hand
G
B♭maj7
I just can't re - mem - ber who to send it to.
And I won't make it an - y oth - er way.
Chorus:
F
F/E
Dm7
G7
C
I've seen fire and I've seen rain
I've seen

F
F/E
Dm7
G7
C
sun - ny days that I thought would nev - er end
I've seen
F
F/E
Dm7
G7
C
lone - ly times when I could not find a friend
But I
B♭
F/A
Gm7
C9
al - ways thought that I'd see you a - gain.
1,2
C9
2nd time to Verse 3
2. Won't you
3. Now I'm
Fine
C9

Verse 3:
C
Gm7/C
F/C
C
walk-ing my mind to an eas-y time my back turned towards_the sun__
G/C
B♭/C
Lord knows when the cold wind blows it-'ll turn your head_ a-round__ Well, there's
C
Gm7/C
F/C
C
hours of time_ on the tel-e-phone line_ to talk a-bout things to come__
G/C
B♭/C
D.S. al Fine
Sweet dreams and fly - ing ma-chines in pie - ces on__ the ground.

HOW CAN YOU MEND A BROKEN HEART

Words and Music by BARRY GIBB
and ROBIN GIBB

F#
B
I was nev - er told a - bout the sor - row.
no one said a word a - bout the sor - row.
Emaj7
And how can you mend a bro - ken heart?
3
mp
F#m7
A
B
How can you stop the rain from fall - ing down? How can you stop
A
B
F#m7
B
E
the sun from shin - ing? What makes the world go 'round?

Emaj7
F#m7
How can you mend this bro-ken man? How can a los-er ev-er
A
B
A
B
win? Please help me mend my bro - ken heart
F#m7
B
1.
E
and let me live a - gain.
2.
E
Emaj7
gain.
rit.

I WILL SURVIVE

Words and Music by DINO FEKARIS
and FREDDIE PERREN

Am
Dm
G
back from out - er space. I just walk in to find you here with that sad
me, some-bod - y new, I'm not that chained up lit - tle per - son still in
Cmaj7
Fmaj7
Bm7-5
look up - on your face. I should have changed that stup-id lock, I should have made you leave your key, if I'd - 've
love with you. And so you felt like drop-pin' in and just ex - pect me to be free. Well now, I'm
E7 (sus)
E7
Am
known for just one sec - ond you'd be back to both - er me. Go on, now
sav - in' all my lov - in' for some - one who's lov - in' me. Go on, now
go, walk out the
Dm
G
Cmaj7
door; just turn a - round, now, 'cause you're not wel - come an - y - more.

Fmaj7
Bm7-5
E7 (sus)
Weren't you the one who tried to hurt me with good-bye? Did you think I'd crum-ble, did you think I'd
(break)
E7
Am
Dm
lay down and die. Oh no, not I, I will sur - vive. Oh, as
G
Cmaj7
Fmaj7
long as I know how to love, I know I'll stay a - live. I've got all my life to live, I've got
Bm7-5
E7 (sus)
E7
Second time D.S. and fade
all my love to give and I'll sur - vive, I will sur - vive! (2.) It took
(D.S.) Now

I FEEL THE EARTH MOVE

Words and Music by
CAROLE KING

1.
Dm7
(C Bass)
Ab
(Bb Bass)
Ebmaj7
Fm
Gm
Abmaj7
Ooh, ba - by, when I see your face,
Fm7
Ab
(Bb Bass)
Ebmaj7
Fm
Gm
Abmaj7
mel-low as the month of May, oh, dar - lin', I can't stand
Fm7
Ab
(Bb Bass)
F
(G Bass)
it when you look at me that (-a) way. I feel the
2.
Dm7
(C Bass)
Cm7
F6

Cm7
F
(C Bass)
Cm7
F7
Cm7
F
(C Bass)
Cm7
F7
Cm7
(add F no D)
F9
Cm7
F7
3
Cm7
F7
Cm7

F7
Ab
(Bb Bass)
Ebmaj7
Abmaj7
Ooh, dar - lin', when you're near me and you ten -
Fm7
Ab
(Bb Bass)
Ebmaj7
Fm
Gm
Abmaj7
der - ly call my name, I know that my e - mo -
Fm7
Ab
(BbBass)
F
(G Bass)
tions are some-thing I just can't tame. I've just got to have you
Cm7
(C Bass)
F
Cm7
(C Bass)
F
Cm7
ba - by. Ah, ah, ah, ah, ah, ah, yeah !

(C Bass)
F
Cm7
(C Bass)
F
Cm7
F
(C Bass)
I feel the earth move un - der my feet; I feel the
Cm7
F
(C Bass)
Cm7
sky tum-bl-in' down, a - tum-bl - in' down. I feel the earth move un -
F
(C Bass)
Cm7
To Coda
F
(C Bass)
der my feet; I feel the sky tum-bl - in' down, a -tum-bl - in' down. I just (-a)
Cm7
F7
Cm7
lose con-trol, down to my ver - y soul.

F7
Cm7
F7
I get (-a) hot and cold all o -
ver, all o - ver, all o - ver, all o - ver. I feel the
Cm7
F
(C Bass)
D.S. al Coda
p
mf
f
Dm7
(C Bass)
Cm7
-tum- bl - in' down, a - tum - bl - in' down, a - tum - bl - in' down,
Coda
rit.
B♭maj7
(C Bass)
A♭maj7
(C Bass)
B♭maj7
(C Bass)
a - tum-bl - in'down, tum-bl- in' down.
Gradually

I WRITE THE SONGS

Words and Music by
BRUCE JOHNSTON

G7sus
G7
Gm7/C
C7
F
Fmaj7
mu - sic, and I write the songs.
young a - gain, e-ven though I'm ver - y old.
I write the songs that make the
Gm7
C7
Gm7
C7
F
Am7/E
whole world sing; I write the songs of love and spe - cial things.
Dm
Dm(#7)
Dm7
G7sus
G7
I write the songs that make the young girls cry;
Gm7/C
1 F
B♭m/F
F
I write the songs, I write the songs.

2
F
E7sus
E7
Oh, my mu - sic makes you dance and gives you
Em7
E7
A
A/G#
spir - it to take a chance,
And I wrote some rock 'n' roll so
F#m
A/E
G7sus
G7
you can move.
Mu - sic fills your heart, well, that's a
G7sus
G7
Gm7/C
C
Gm7/C
C
real fine place to start,
It's from me, it's for you, it's from you, it's for me, it's a world-

Gm7/C
C
Gm7/C
C
A
Amaj7
Bm7
- wide_ sym-pho-ny._
I write the songs_ that make the whole world sing,
E7
A
F#m
F#m(#7)
F#m7
I write the songs_ of love and spe - cial things,_
I write the songs_ that make the
A/B
B7
Bm7/E
F#m
F#m(#7)
F#m7
young girls cry,_
I write the songs_ I write the songs._
A/B
B7
Bm7/E
A
I am mu - sic and I write the songs._
Ped.

IF

Words and Music by
DAVID GATES

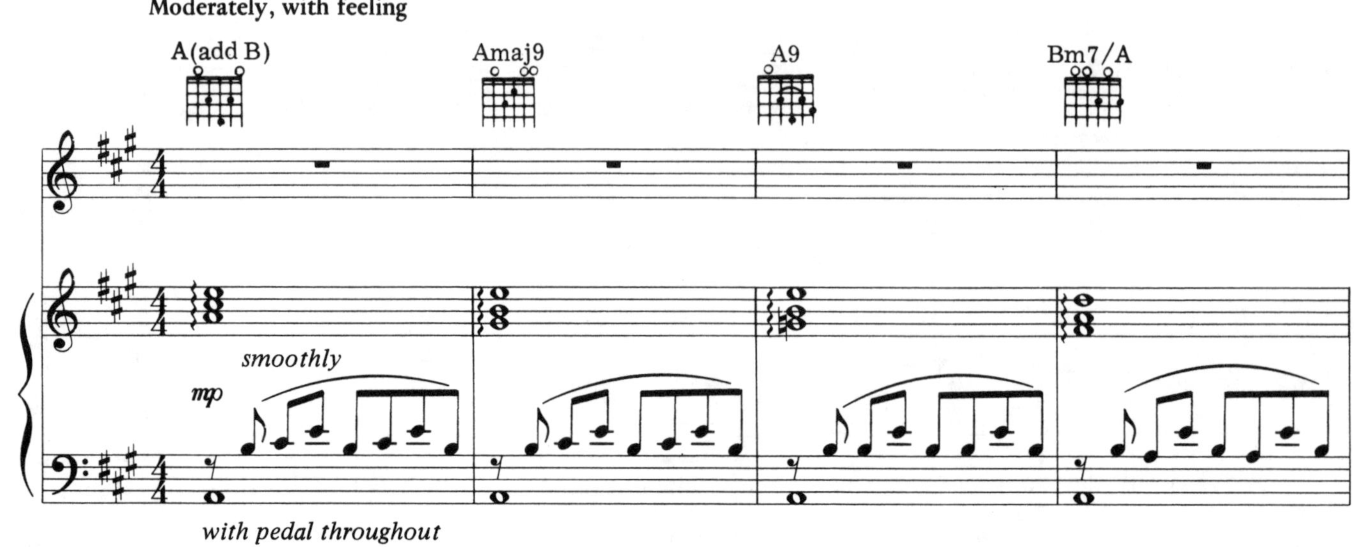

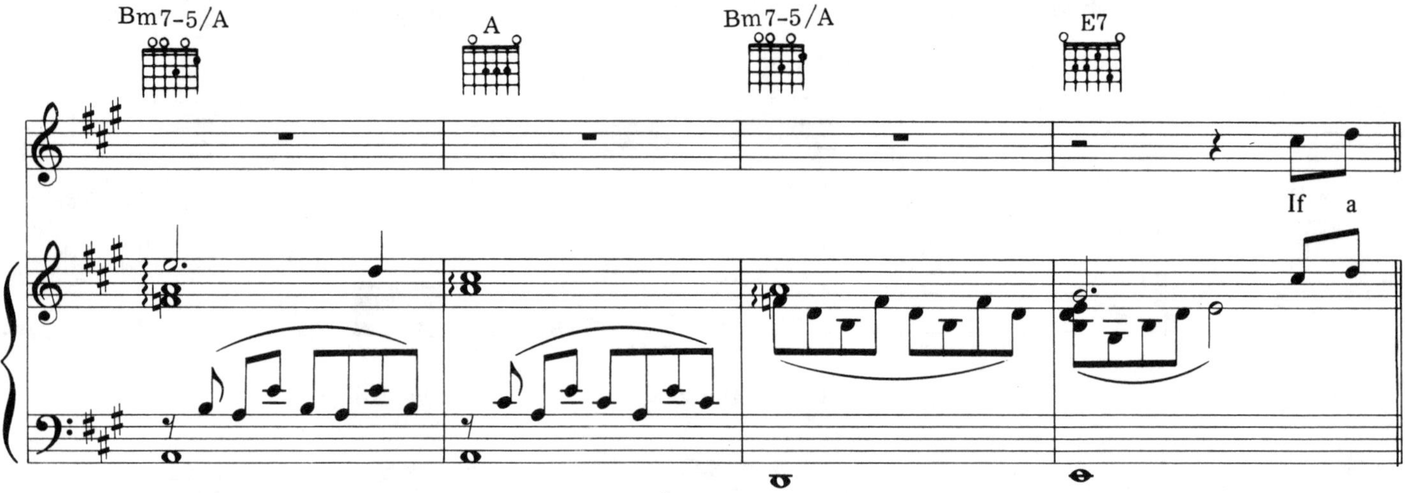

Bm7/A
Bm7-5/A
A
Bm7-5/D
you? The words will nev-er show the you I've come to know.
you; to-mor-row and to-day, be-side you all the way.
E7
A(add B)
Amaj9
A9
If a face could launch a thou-sand ships, then where am I to go?
If the world should stop re-volv-ing, spin-ning slow-ly down to die,
Bm7/A
Bm7-5/A
A
Bm7-5/D
There's no one home but you. You're all that's left me
I'd spend the end with you. And when the world was

E7
F♯m
F♯m/E♯
to. And when my love for life
through, then one by one the stars
F♯m/E
D6
C♯m7-5
is run-ning dry, you come and pour
would all go out. Then you and I
F♯7
1.
Bm7
E7
your-self on me. If a
would
2.
Bm7
sim-ply
D/E
A
Bm7/F♯
3fr.
Bm7-5/F
3fr.
A
fly a-way.
rit.
a tempo

IMAGINE

Words and Music by
JOHN LENNON

F
C
Cmaj7
a-bove us
on - ly sky.
F
Am/E
Im-ag-ine
all
the
peo -
Dm7
F/C
G
C/G
ple
liv - ing
for
to - day.
G7
C
Cmaj7
Ah.
Im - ag - ine there's
no
coun -

F
C
Cmaj7
tries.
ions.
It is - n't hard to do.
I won - der if you can.
Noth - ing to kill or die
No need for greed or hun -
for
ger,
and no re - li - gion, too.
a broth - er - hood of man.
3

F
Am/E
Im - ag - ine all the peo -
Im - ag - ine all the peo -
Dm7
F/C
G
C/G
ple living life in peace.
ple sharing all the world.
G7
F
G
You you may say I'm a
C
E7
F
G
dream - er. But I'm not the on - ly one.

C
E7
F
G
I hope some day you'll
C
E7
1
F
G
join us
and the world will
C
Cmaj7
be as one.
Im - ag - ine no pos - ses -
2
F
G
C
and the world will live as one.
rit.

IT NEVER RAINS
(IN SOUTHERN CALIFORNIA)

Words and Music by ALBERT HAMMOND
and MICHAEL HAZELWOOD

Am7 D G C6 G
-ies rang true, sure rang true.
Am7 D G
Seems It Nev-er Rains In South-ern Cal-i-for-nia, Seems I've of-
Am7 D G Am7
-ten heard that kind of talk be-fore. It nev-er rains in Cal-i-for-
D G Em Am7 D
-nia, But girl, don't they warn ya, it pours man, it pours.

G
C6
G
Am7
D
Out of work, I'm out a' my head, Out of self re-
spect, I'm out a' bread. I'm un-der-loved, I'm un-der-fed. I wan-na go home.
Em
It nev-er rains in Cal-i-for-nia, But girl, don't they warn ya, It pours, man, it pours. Will you

Am7
D
G
tell the folks back home I near-ly made it, Had of-
Am7
D
G
C
G
-fers but don't know which one to take. Please don't
Am7
D
G
Em
3
tell them how you found me, Don't tell them how you found me Give me a
3
Am7
D
G
C6
G
D.S. and Fade
break, Give me a break. Seems it

IT'S IMPOSSIBLE
(SOMOS NOVIOS)

English Lyric by SID WAYNE
Spanish Words and Music by ARMANDO MANZANERO

Dm7
G7
Bm7♭5
ba - by not to cry, it's just im - pos - si - ble.
na - mos lo más gran - de de es - te mun - do.
E7
Am7
Cm
Can I hold you clos - er to me, and not
Nos a - ma - mos nos be - sa - mos co - mo
G
E7♭9
Am
feel you go - ing through me? Split the sec - ond that I
no - vios nos de - sea - mos y has - ta a ve - ces sin mo -
A7
D7
nev - er think of you? Oh, how im - pos - si - ble.
ti - vo sin ra - zón nos e - no - ja - mos.

Am7
D7
G
G6
Gmaj7
G6
Can the o - cean _ keep from rush-ing to the shore? It's just im -
So - mos no - vios _ man - te - ne - mos un ca - ri - ño lim - pio y
F#m7♭5
B7
Em
pos - si - ble. If I had you, _ could I
pu - ro. Co - mo to - dos _ pro - cu -
Dm7
G7
Bm7♭5
E7
ev - er want for more? It's just im - pos - si - ble. And to -
ra - mos el mo - men - to más os - cu - ro pa - ra ha-
Am7
Cm
mor - row, _ should you ask me for the world, some - how I'd
blar - nos _ pa - ra dar - nos el más dul - ce de los

G
E7♭9
get it.
I would sell my ver - y soul and not re -
be - sos
re - cor - dar de que co - lor son los ce -
Am
D7
G
gret it,
for to live with-out your love is just im - pos - si - ble.
re - zos
Sin ha - cer más co - men - ta - rios so - mos no - vios.
C♯m7♭5
D7
no chord
G
Em7
It's im - pos - si - ble.
Im - pos - si - ble.
So - mos no - vios
somos no - vios
Am7
D7
G
Cm6
G
Mm,
im - pos - si - ble.
siem - pre no - vios.
rall.

IT'S TOO LATE

Words by TONI STERN
Music by CAROLE KING

B♭maj7
Fmaj7
B♭maj7
Fmaj7
real-ly did try to make it. Some-thin' in-side has died and I can't hide
1.2.
Dm7
Fmaj7
E7sus
Em7
Am7
D6
Am7
And I just can't fake it.
D6
3.
Dm7
Fmaj7
G7sus
G7
Cmaj7
2. It And I just can't fake it. It's too late, ba-
3.
Fmaj7
Cmaj7
Fmaj7
Cmaj7
-by, It's too late now, dar - lin', It's too late.

JUST THE WAY YOU ARE

Words and Music by
BILLY JOEL

D/F♯
Bm7
Bm7/E
E9
G/A
you're too fa-mil - iar
And I don't see you an - y more
D
Bm6
Gmaj7
Bm
D7
I would not leave you
in times of trou - ble
Gmaj7
Gm
D/F♯
Am
D7
Gmaj7
We nev-er could have come this far
mm mm
I took the good
Gm6
D/F♯
Bm7
Em7
G/A
times
I'll take the bad times
I'll take you just the way you are

D
Gm
G/D
D
Gm6
G/D
D
Bm6
Gmaj7
Bm
D7
Gmaj7
Don't go try - ing Some new fash - ion Don't change the col -
D/F♯
Am7
D7
Gmaj7
Gm
or of your hair mm mm You al - ways have my
Bm7
Bm7/E
E9
un - spok - en pas - sion Al - though I might not seem to care

G/A
D
Bm6
Gmaj7
I don't want clever conversation
Bm
D7
Gmaj7
Gm
D/F♯
Am7
D7
I never want to work that hard mm mm
Gmaj7
Gm
D/F♯
Bm7
Em7
I just want someone that I can talk to
I want you just the way you are.
G/A
D
Gm6/D
G/D
D
Gm6/D
D
D7

G A F♯m7 B7 Em7
I need to know that you will al - ways be The same old some-
A D Am/C Bb C
one that I knew Oh What will it take till you be - lieve
Am7 D D7 Gm7 C G/A
in me The way that I be - lieve in you
D Bm6 Gmaj7 Bm D7
I said I love you and that's for - ev - er
voice tacet on D.S.
instrumental on D.S.

Gmaj7
Gm
Gm6
D/F♯
Am7
D7
Gmaj7
And this I prom-ise from the heart
mm mm I could not love
Gm6
D/F♯
Bm7
Em7
G/A
you any-y bet-ter
I love you just the way you are
D
Gm6
G/D
D
Gm6
G/D
D
D.S. al Coda
CODA
D/E
E9
G/A
D
I don't want

Bm6
G7
Bm
D7
Gmaj7
Gm
clev - er
con - ver - sa - tion
I nev - er
want to work that hard
D/F♯
Am7
D7
Gmaj7
Gm6
D/F
mm
I just want
some - one
that I can talk
Bm7
Em7
G/A
Bb
C
to
I want you
just
the way you are
Am7
D7
Gm7
A7
Dmaj7
Whoa

LET IT BE

Words and Music by JOHN LENNON
and PAUL McCARTNEY

Am
G
F
C
G
standing right in front of me
Speak-ing words of wis - dom, Let it
F
C/E
Dm7
C
Am
G
be.
Let it be, let it be, let it be,
Let it be, let it be, let it be,
F
C
G
let it be,
Whis-per words of wis - dom, Let it be.
let it be,
Whis-per words of wis - dom, Let it be.
F
C/E
Dm7
C
G
And when the bro - ken-heart - ed peo-ple
And when the night is cloud - y there is

Am G F C G
liv-ing in the world a-gree There will be an an-swer, Let it
still a light that shines on me Shine un-til to-mor-row. Let it
F C/E Dm7 C G
be. For though they may be part-ed there is
be. I wake up to the sound of mu-sic
Am G F C G
still a chance that they will see There will be an an-swer, Let it
Moth-er Mar-y comes to me Speak-ing words of wis-dom, Let it
F C/E Dm7 C Am G
be. Let it be, let it be, let it be,
be.

F
C
G
let it be,
There will be an an - swer,
Let it be.
F
C/E
Dm7
C
G
Am
G
Let it be,
let it be,
let it be,
F
C
G
To Coda
let it be,
Whis - per words of wis - dom, let it be.
There will be an an - swer, let it be.
F
C/E
Dm7
C
F
Em
Dm7
C
B♭
F/A

G F C F C G F C
D.S. al Coda
CODA
F C/E Dm7 C Am G
Let it be, let it be, let it be,
F C G
let it be. Whis-per words of wis - dom, let it be.
F C/E Dm7 C F Em Dm7 C B♭ F/A G F C

MAGGIE MAY

Words and Music by ROD STEWART
and MARTIN QUITTENTON

Em
F#m
Em7
Maggie, I couldn't have tried any more.
You
Em
A
Em
A
lured me a-way from home, just to save you from be-ing a - lone.
You
Em
A
D
stole my heart and that's what real - ly hurts.
The
A
G
D
morn - ing sun, when it's in your face, real - ly shows your age,
But
A
G
D
G
that don't wor-ry me none in my eyes you're ev - 'ry - thing.
I laughed at all of your

2. You lured me away from home, just to save you from being alone.
You stole my soul, that's a pain I can do without.
All I needed was a friend to lend a guiding hand.
But you turned into a lover, and, Mother, what a lover! You wore me out.
All you did was wreck my bed, and in the morning kick me in the head.
Oh, Maggie, I couldn't have tried any more.

3. You lured me away from home, 'cause you didn't want to be alone.
You stole my heart, I couldn't leave you if I tried.
I suppose I could collect my books and get back to school.
Or steal my Daddy's cue and make a living out of playing pool,
Or find myself a rock and roll band that needs a helpin' hand.
Oh, Maggie, I wish I'd never seen your face. **(To Coda)**

MANDY

Words and Music by SCOTT ENGLISH
and RICHARD KERR

Ab
F7
Bb
Gm
Eb
never re - a - lized how hap-py you made me.
tears are in my mind and noth-in' is rhym - ing.
cry - ing on a breeze the pain is call - ing.
Oh, Man - dy well, you came and you gave with-out tak -
F
F7
Bb
Gm
Eb
- ing. But I sent you a - way. Oh, Man - dy well, you kissed me and stopped me from shak -
F
F7
To Coda
1
Bb
Gm
Eb
- ing, and I need you to - day. Oh, Man - dy!
F7
2
Gm
Dm
Eb
I'm Man - dy

Cm7
F7
D.S. al Coda
CODA
C
Man - dy well, you came
Am
F
G
G7
and you gave with - out tak - ing, but I sent you a - way. Oh Man -
C
Am
F
G
G7
- dy, well you kissed me and stopped me from shak - ing, and I need
C
Am
F
G
F/G
Repeat and Fade
you.

ME AND BOBBY McGEE

Words and Music by KRIS KRISTOFFERSON
and FRED FOSTER

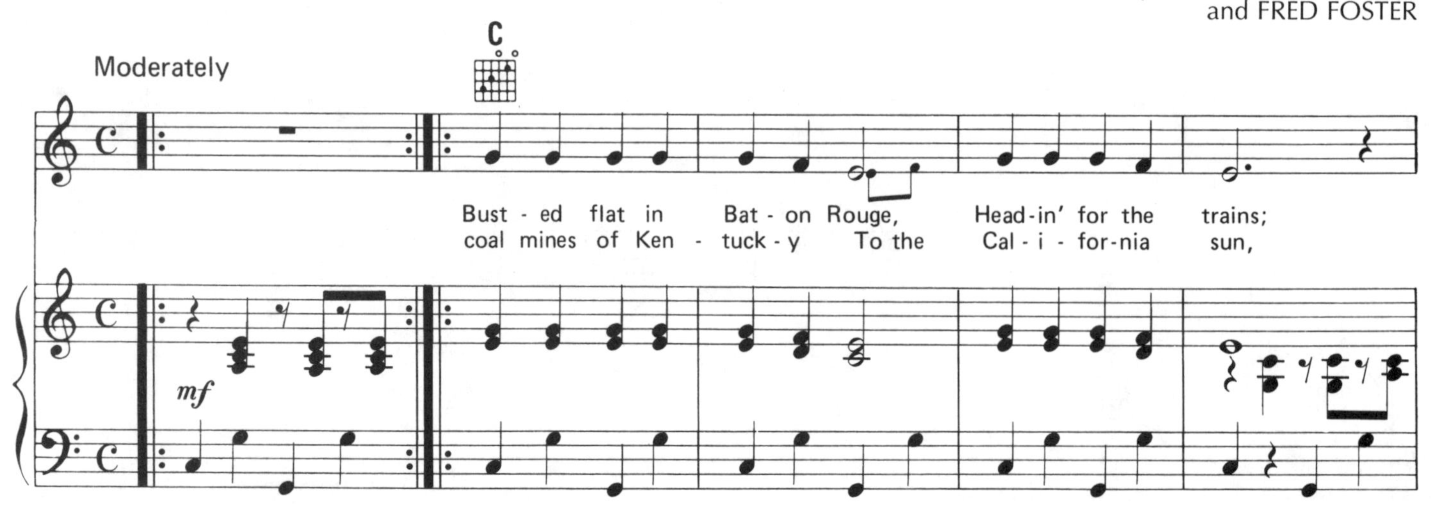

C
way to New Or - leans.
kept me from the cold.
I took my har - poon out of my
Then some - where near Sa - lin - as, Lord, I
C7
F
dir - ty, red ban - dan - na And was blow - in' sad while Bob - by sang the blues;
let her slip a - way Look - in' for the home I hope she'll find;
C
With them wind - shield wi - pers slap - pin' time and Bob - by clap - pin' hands We fin - 'ly
And I'd trade all of my to - mor - rows for a sin - gle yes - ter - day,
G7
C
F
sang up ev - 'ry song that driv - er knew.
Hold - in' Bob - by's bod - y next to mine.
Free - dom's just an - oth - er word for
Free - dom's just an - oth - er word for

C
G7
C
noth - in' left to lose, Noth - in' ain't worth noth - in', but it's free;
noth - in' left to lose, Noth - in' left is all she left for me;
F
C
Feel - in' good was eas - y, Lord, When Bob - by sang the blues;
G7
And feel - in' good was good e - nough for me,
And, bud - dy, that was good e - nough for me,
Good e - nough for
1
C
2
C
me and Bob - by Mc - Gee.
From the
Gee.

NADIA'S THEME
from THE YOUNG AND THE RESTLESS

By BARRY DeVORZON
and PERRY BOTKIN, JR.

1.
2.
mf
decresc.

mp a tempo
L.H.
L.H.
L.H.
molto rit.
R.H.
R.H.

MIDNIGHT TRAIN TO GEORGIA

Words and Music by
JIM WEATHERLY

F
Am/E
Gm/D
B♭/C
F
Am/E
He said he's go - in' back to find
ooh, what's left
Gm/D
B♭/C
F
Am/E
Gm/D
Dm7/G
of his world,
the world he left be-hind
not so long
B♭/C
F
Am
a - go.
He's leav - in'
B♭
B♭/C
F
Am
B♭
B♭/C
on that mid-night train to Geor - gia,
And he's

F
Am
Dm7
Dm7/G
B♭/C
go - in' back
to a sim - pler place and time.
F
Am
B♭
B♭/C
And I'll be with him
on that mid-night train to
Dm7
Dm7/G
B♭
Geor - gia
I'd rath-er live in this world
3
B♭/C
F
Am/E
Gm/D
B♭/C
than live with - out him in mine.

F
Am/E
Gm/D
B♭/C
F
Am/E
He kept dream - in' that some - day he'd be a star,
Gm/D
B♭/C
F
Am/E
Gm/D
Dm7/G
But he sure found out the hard way that dreams don't
B♭/C
F
Am/E
al - ways come true. So he pawned all his
Gm/D
B♭/C
F
Am/E
Gm/D
B♭/C
hopes and he e - ven sold his old car; bought a

F
Am/E
Gm/D
Dm7/G
B♭/C
one - way tick-et to the life he once knew. Oh, yes he did!
F
Am
B♭
B♭/C
He said he would be leav - in' on that mid - night train to
F
Am
B♭
B♭/C
F
Am
Geor - gia, And he's go - in' back
Dm7
Dm7/G
B♭/C
to a sim - pler place and time.

F
Am
B♭
B♭/C
And I'll be with him on that mid - night train to
Dm7
Dm7/G
B♭
Geor - gia;
I'd rath - er live in his world
3
B♭/C
F
Am/E
Gm/D
B♭/C
than live with - out him in mine.
F
Am/E
Gm/D
B♭/C
Repeat and Fade
Go, gon - na board, gon - na board, gon - na board the mid - night train. Got - ta

PIANO MAN

Words and Music by
BILLY JOEL

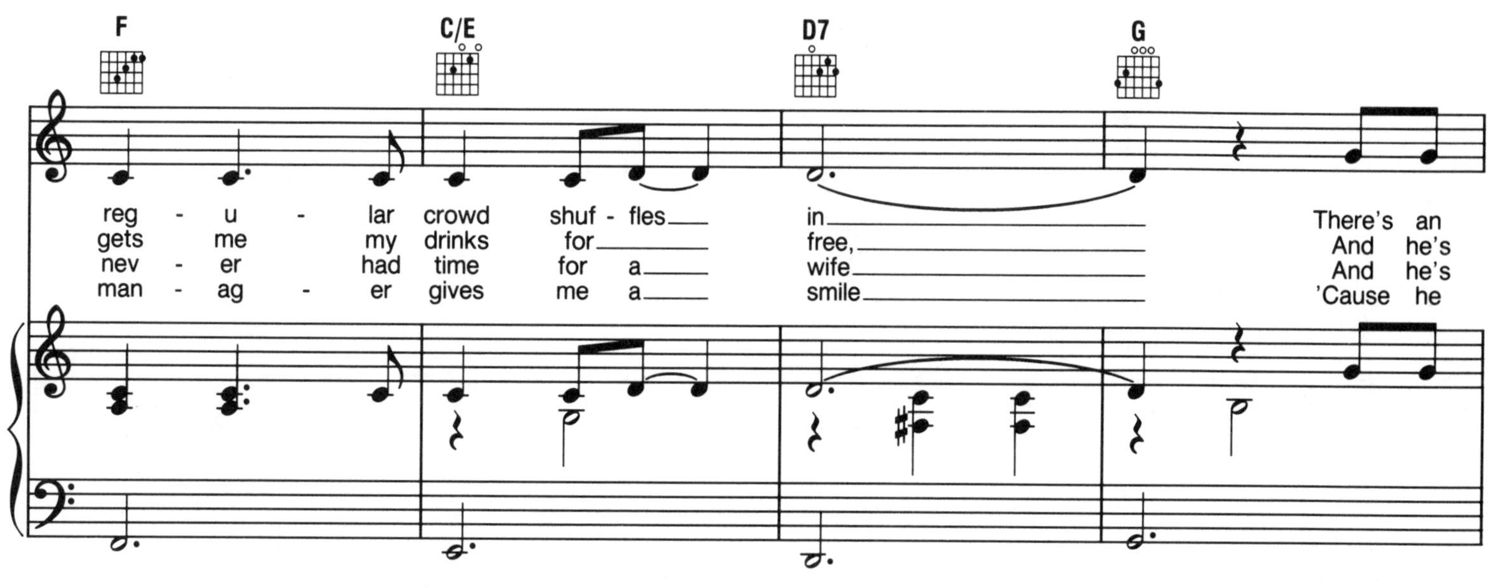
F
C/E
D7
G
reg - u - lar crowd shuf - fles in There's an
gets me my drinks for free, And he's
nev - er had time for a wife And he's
man - ag - er gives me a smile 'Cause he

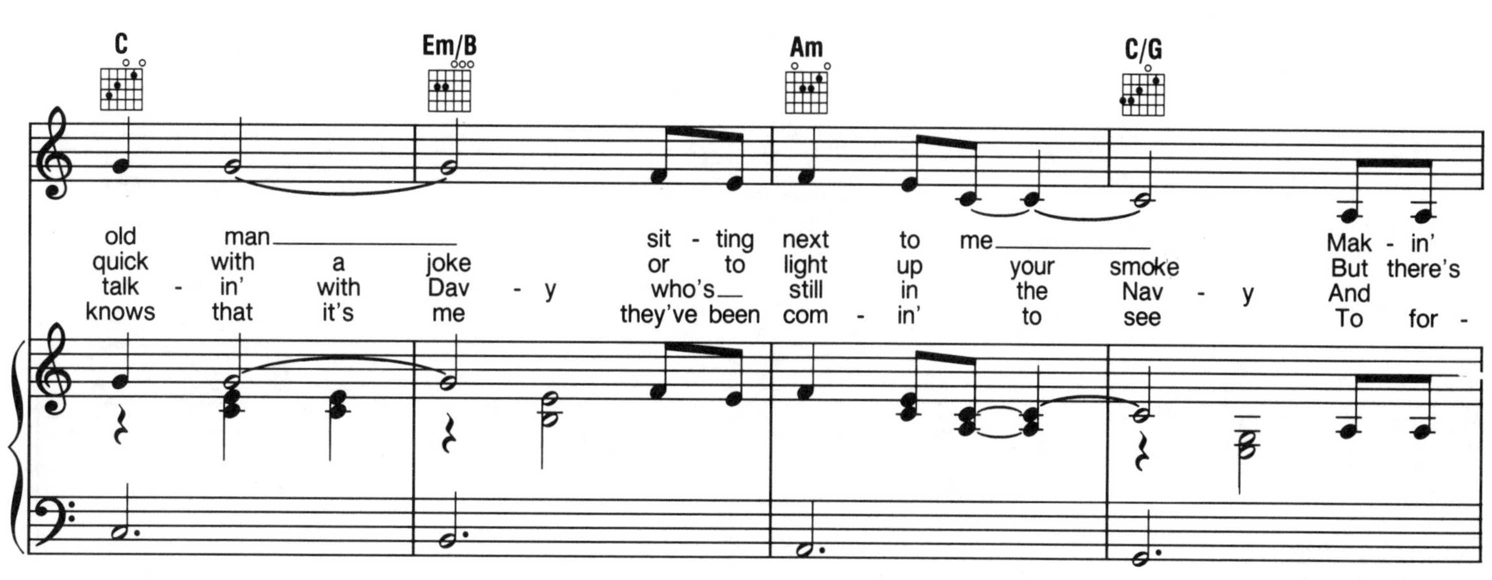
C
Em/B
Am
C/G
old man sit - ting next to me Mak - in'
quick with a joke or to light up your smoke But there's
talk - in' with Dav - y who's still in the Nav - y And
knows that it's me they've been com - in' to see To for -

F
G11
C
F/C
Cmaj7
love to his ton - ic and gin.
some - place that he'd rath - er be.
prob - ab - ly will be for life.
get - a - bout life for a while.

G11 C Em/B Am C/G
3
He says, "Son, can you play me a mem-o-ry? I'm
He says, "Bill, I be-lieve this is kill-ing me," As a
And the wait-ress is prac-tic-ing pol-i-tics, As the
And the pia-no sounds like a car-ni-val And the

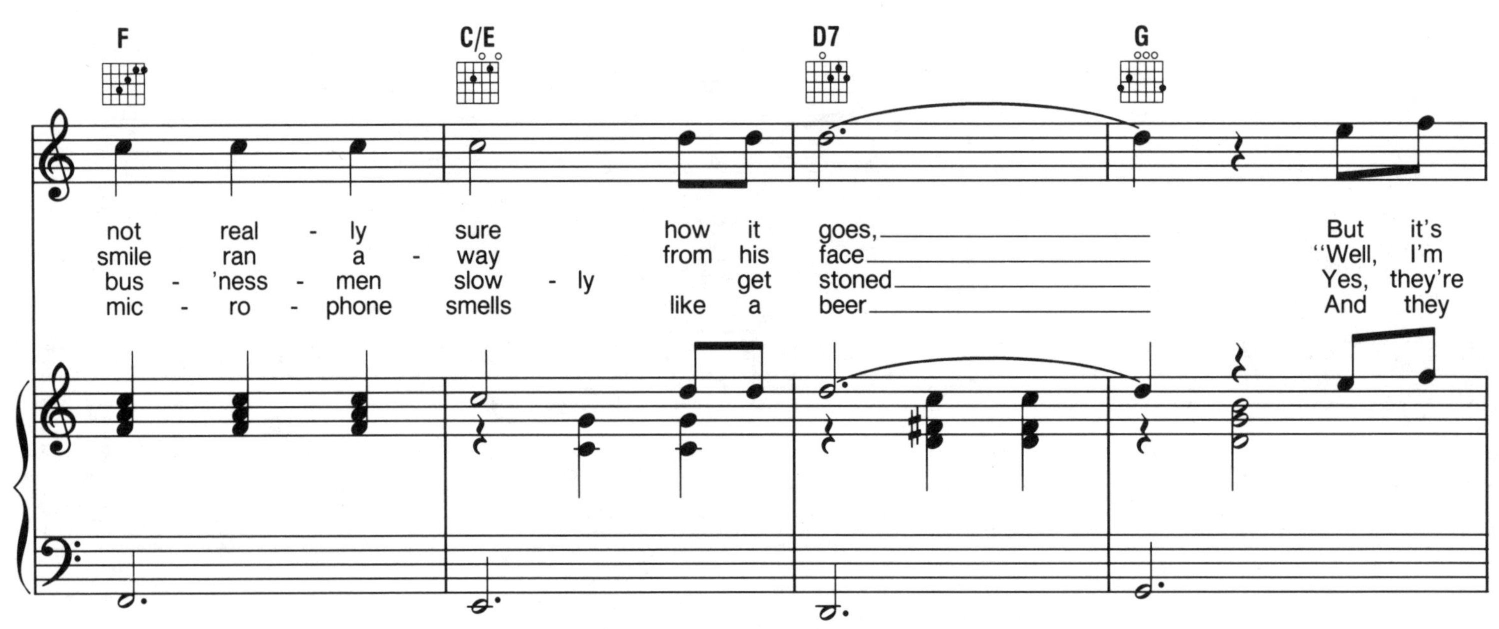
F C/E D7 G
not real-ly sure how it goes, But it's
smile ran a-way from his face "Well, I'm
bus-'ness-men slow-ly get stoned Yes, they're
mic-ro-phone smells like a beer And they

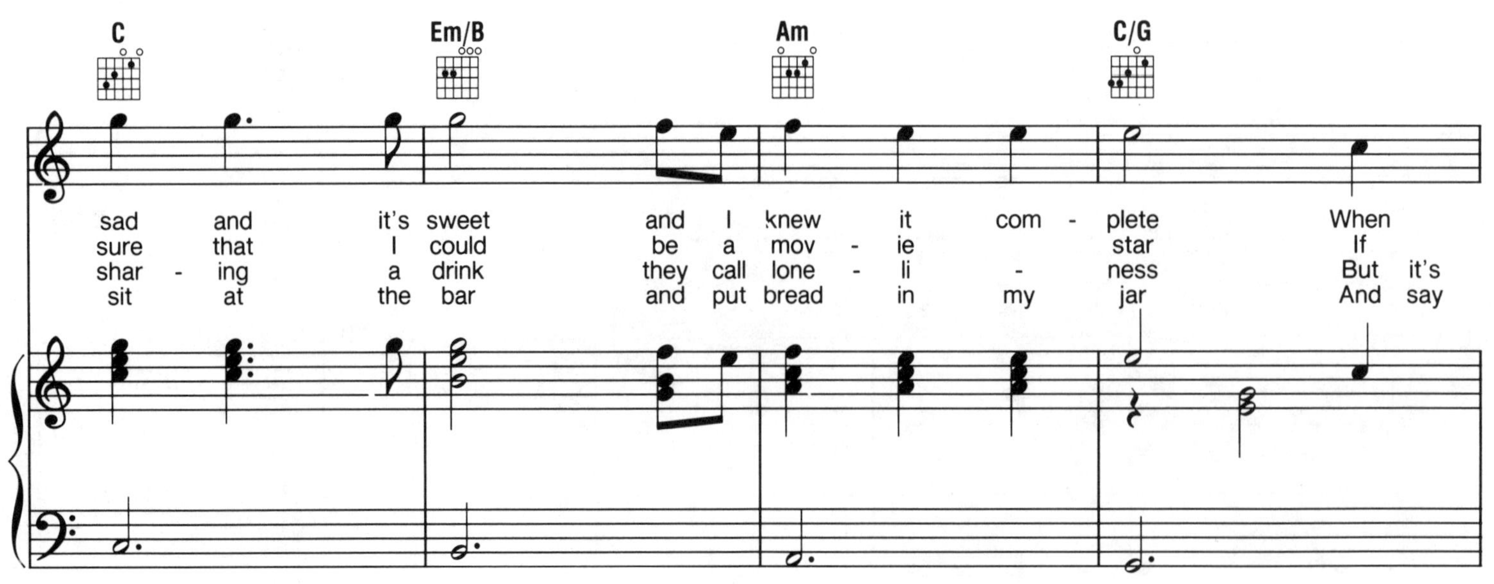
C Em/B Am C/G
sad and it's sweet and I knew it com-plete When
sure that I could be a mov-ie star If
shar-ing a drink they call lone-li-ness But it's
sit at the bar and put bread in my jar And say

F
G11
C
Am
I wore a young - er man's clothes.''
I could get out of this place.''
bet - ter than drink - in' a - lone.
''Man what are you do -in' here?''
Da da da
Da da da
Instrumental
Da da da
mp

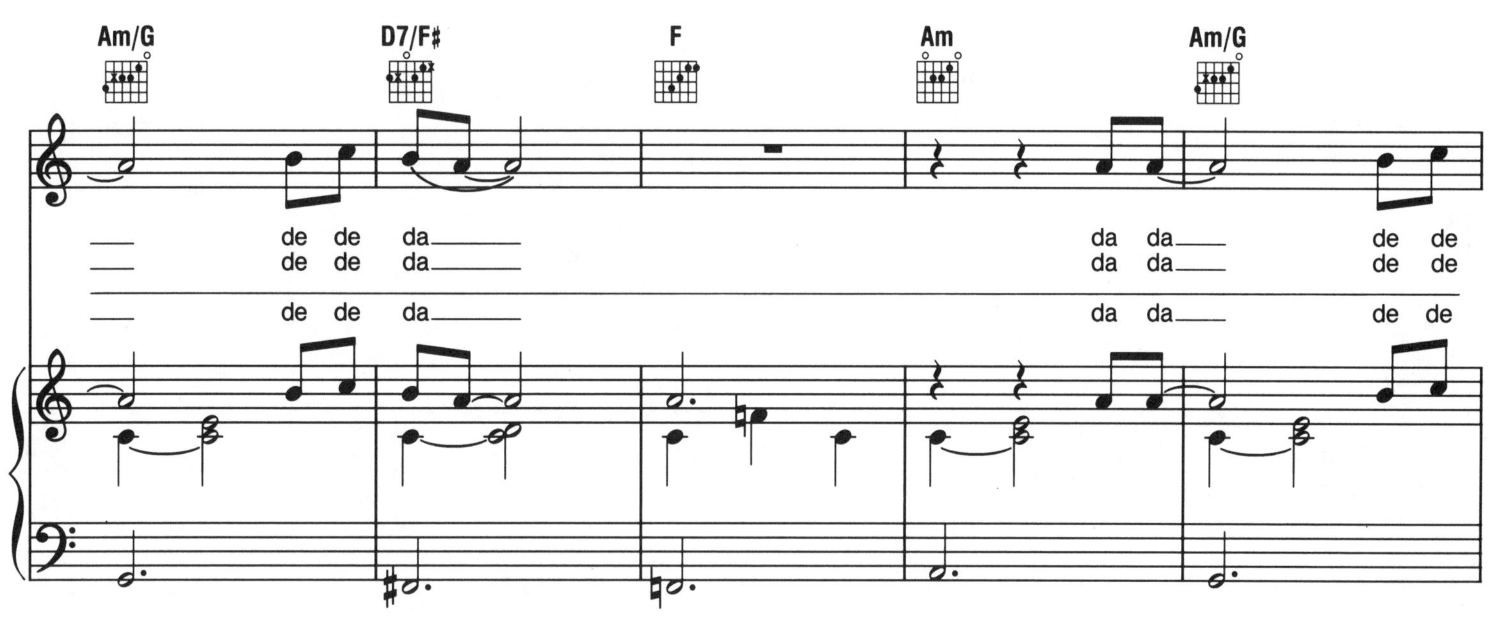
Am/G
D7/F♯
F
Am
Am/G
de de da
da da
de de

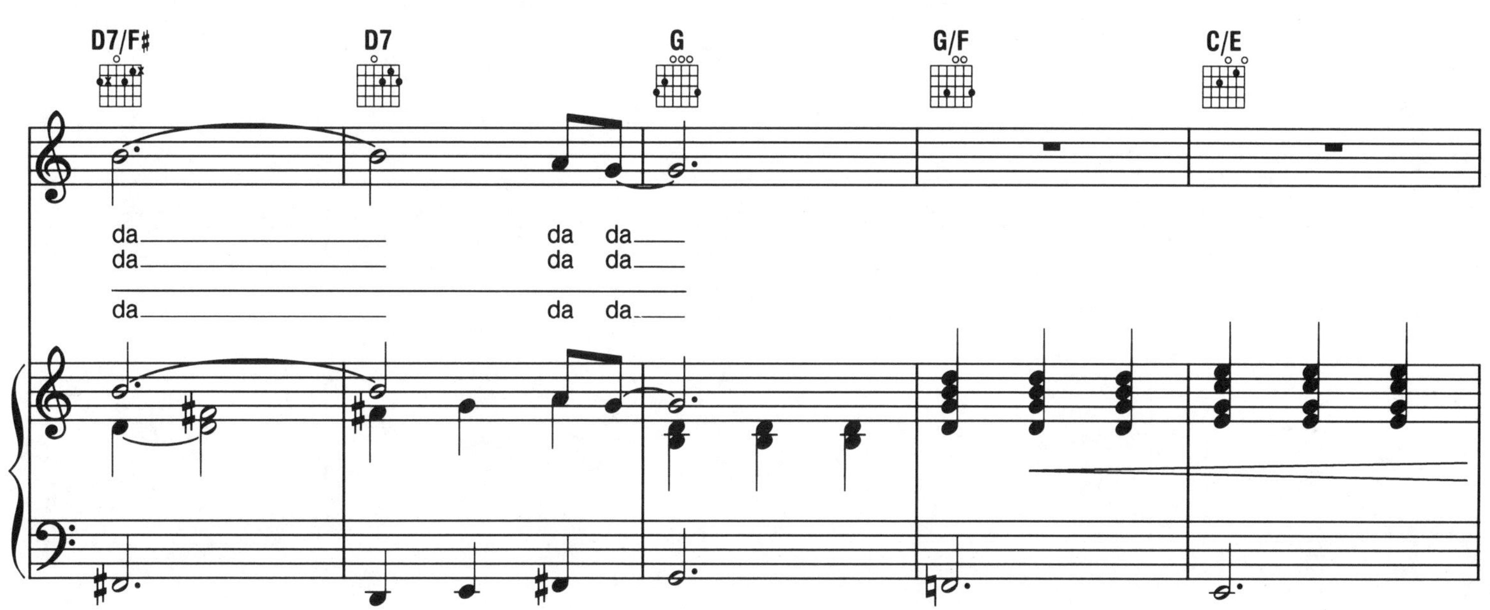
D7/F♯
D7
G
G/F
C/E
da
da da

G7/D
C
Em/B
Am
C/G
Sing us a song, you're the pia - no man
F
C/E
D7
G
C
Sing us a song to - night. Well, we're all in the
Em/B
Am
C/G
F
G11
mood for a mel - o - dy. And you've got us feel - in' al -
C
F/C
Cmaj7
1,2,3
G11
4
G11
D.C. al Fine
right.
2. Now
3. Now
4. It's a

STAYIN' ALIVE

from SATURDAY NIGHT FEVER

Words and Music by BARRY GIBB,
MAURICE GIBB and ROBIN GIBB

Medium Rock beat

f

Well, you can tell

Fm7 Eb Fm

by the way I use my walk, I'm a wom - an's man; no time to talk.
get low and I get high, and if I can't get ei - ther, I real - ly try. Got the

Fm7 Eb Fm

Mu - sic loud and wom - en warm, I've been kicked a - round since I was born. And now it's
wings of heav - en on my shoes. I'm a danc - in' man and I just can't lose. You know it's

Bb7
all right. It's O K. And you may look the oth - er way.
all right. It's O K. I'll live to see an - oth - er day.
We can try to un - der - stand the New York Times' ef - fect on man.
Fm7
Wheth-er you're a broth-er or wheth - er you're a moth-er, you're stay - in' a - live, stay - in' a - live.
Feel the cit - y break-in' and ev - 'ry-bod - y shak - in', and we're stay-in' a - live, stay - in' a - live.

Ah, ha, ha, ha, stay-in' a-live, stay-in' a-live. Ah, ha, ha, ha,
Fm
Eb/F
Fm
stay-in' a-live.
Cm7
To Coda
1. Fm7
Well now, I
2. Fm7
Bb7
Life go-in' no-where.

Fm7
Some-bod - y help me.
Some-bod - y help me, yeah.
Bb7
Life go - in' no where.
Some-bod - y help me, yeah.
Fm7
D.S. al Coda (lyric 1)
Stay-in' a - live.
Well, you can tell
CODA
Fm7
Bb7
Life go - in' no - where.

Some - bod - y help me.
Some - bod - y help me, yeah.
Fm7
Bb7
Life go - in' no - where.
Some - bod - y help me, yeah.
Fm7
I'm stay - in' a - live.
Repeat and Fade

PRECIOUS AND FEW

Words and Music by
WALTER D. NIMS

Dmaj7
G♯m7
4fr
C♯7
F♯m7
B7
can't find my way back home
can't hold you in my arms
it just would-n't be fair,
Emaj7
D
A/C♯
Bm7
2fr
E7
'cause pre-cious and few are the mo-ments we two can
1
A
E7
Bm7/F♯
E7/G♯
2
A
share.
share.
B♭maj7
Am7
Gm
3fr
E♭maj7
3fr
3
3

F
F7
E♭maj7
3fr
Am7
D7
And if I can't find my way back home
Gm7
3fr
C7
Fmaj7
E♭
3fr
B♭/D
it just would - n't be fair,
'cause pre-cious and few are the mo -
Cm7
3fr
F7
B♭
B♭/A♭
F♯7
- ments we two can share.
B
C♯m7
4fr
A
F♯
Pre-cious and few are the mo - ments we two can share.

B
C#m7
4fr
A
F#
F#7
Qui-et and blue like the sky I'm hung o-ver you.
And if I
Emaj7
Bbm7
Eb7
G#m7
C#7
can't find my way back home
it just would-n't be fair,
F#maj7
E
B/D#
C#m7
F#7
'cause pre-cious and few are the mo - ments we two can share.
F#7
B
C#m7/B
Bdim
rit.

SPEAK SOFTLY, LOVE
(LOVE THEME)

from the Paramount Picture THE GODFATHER

Words by LARRY KUSIK
Music by NINO ROTA

Bb7/D Bb7 Eb Db/F Fm6/Ab
3fr
6fr
days warmed by the sun, deep vel-vet nights when we are
G
no chord
Cm Fm/C Cm
3fr
3fr
one. Speak soft-ly, love, so no one hears us but the sky. The vows of
Fm/C Cm Fm6/C Cm Fm/C Fm
3fr
6fr
3fr
love we make will live un-til we die. My life is yours and all be-
Cm Cm/G G7sus G7
3fr
3fr
1
Cm
3fr
2
Cm
3fr
cause you came in-to my world with love so soft-ly, love. Speak soft-ly, love.
rit.

THE WAY WE WERE

Words by ALAN and MARILYN BERGMAN
Music by MARVIN HAMLISCH

Dmaj7
E7sus
E7
1
Amaj7
F♯m7
Bm7
D/E
of the way we were.
for the way we
Scat-tered
2
Amaj7
A7
Dmaj7
C♯m7
Bm7
were.
Can it be that it was all so sim-ple then,
C♯m7
F♯7sus
F♯7
Bm7
Bm7/A
or has time re-writ-ten ev-'ry line?
If we had the chance to do it
E7sus
E7
Amaj7
D/E
E7
D.S. al Coda
all a-gain, tell me would we?
Could we?

CODA
Dmaj7
C#7sus
C#7
F#m7
F#m7/E
Dmaj7
we sim-ply choose to for - get. So it's the
C#m7
Dmaj7
C#m7
laugh - ter we will re - mem - ber,
Dmaj7
C#m7
F#m7
Bm7
Bm7/E
when-ev - er we re - mem - ber the way we
Amaj7
Dmaj7
D/E
Amaj7
Dmaj7
Amaj7
were; the way we were.
rit.

YOU NEEDED ME

Words and Music by
RANDY GOODRUM

G7
C
C7
up and gave me dig - ni - ty___ Some-how You Need-ed Me.
lies back in - to truth a - gain_ you ev - en called me friend.
You gave me
F
B♭
C7
strength to stand a - lone a - gain,_ to face the world, out on my
F
F7
B♭
Bdim
own a - gain You put me high up - on a ped - e - stal,_ so
F
A7
Dm
G7
To Coda
C7
high that I___ can al - most see_ e - ter - ni - ty__ You Need - ed Me_ You

F
A7
Dm
F
B♭
F
Need-ed Me.
And I
can't be-lieve it's
you
I
can't be-lieve
it's
true,
I
Gm7
C7
F
A7
Dm
F
need-ed you
and you were
there.
And I'll
nev-er leave why should
I
leave
I'd be
B♭
F
G7
C7
D.S. al Coda
a fool,
'cause I've
fin-'lly found some-one
who real-ly cares
You held my
CODA
G7
C7
F
D7
Gm7
C7
F
Need-ed Me
You Need-ed Me
You
Need-ed Me
You Need-ed Me

YOU MAKE LOVIN' FUN

Words and Music by
CHRISTINE McVIE

E♭
3fr
Gm
3fr
Oh,
You,
can it be so?
you make lov - ing fun.
F
This feel - ing fol - lows me wher - ev - er I go.
And I don't have to tell you you're the on - ly one.
E♭
3fr
To Coda

B♭
I nev - er did be - lieve
B♭/A♭
in mir - a - cles.
Gm7
3 fr
F
E♭
3 fr
But I've a feel-ing it's time to try.
B♭
I nev-er did be - lieve

B♭/A♭
in the ways of mag - ic.
Gm7
3fr
F
But I'm be - gin - ning to won - der why.
E♭
3fr
D.S. al Coda
Don't,
CODA
B♭
You,
F
E♭
3fr
Repeat and Fade
you make lov - ing fun.

YOU'VE GOT A FRIEND

Words and Music by
CAROLE KING

Gm7
3fr
C7
Fm
C7
close your eyes and think of me and soon I will be there
keep your head to - geth - er and call my name out loud;
Fm/A♭
C7/G
Fm
B♭m7
Cm7
3fr
to bright - en up e - ven your dark - est night.
soon you'll hear me knock-in' at your door.
B♭m7/E♭
6fr
E♭
3fr
B♭m7/E♭
6fr
no chord
A♭
4fr
You just call out my name
D♭
and you know wher-ev - er I am I'll come run -

A♭
B♭m7/E♭
- nin' to see you a - gain.
A♭
A♭maj7
Win-ter, spring, sum-mer or fall,
D♭
A♭6
A♭7
To Coda
1
D♭
Cm7
all you have to do is call and I'll be there.
B♭m7 B♭m7/E♭
A♭
D♭/A♭
You've got a friend.
4fr
6fr
3fr

Db
Ab/C
Bbm
Ab
Gm7
C7
no chord
2
Db
Cm7
If the sky there, yes, I will.
Bbm7
Bbm7/Eb
Gb
Db
Now ain't it good to know that you've got a friend when
Ab
Abmaj7
Db
peo-ple can be so cold? They'll hurt you, yes, and de-sert
Gb7
Fm
Bb7
you and take your soul if you let them. Oh, but

Bbm7/Eb
6fr
no chord
D.S. al Coda
don't you let them.
You just call
CODA
Db
Cm7
3fr
Bbm7
Bbm7/Eb
6fr
there, yes, I will.
You've got a friend.
Ab
4fr
Db/Ab
4fr
You've got a
Ab
4fr
Db/Ab
4fr
Repeat and Fade
friend.
Ain't it good to know you've got a

YOUR SONG

Words and Music by ELTON JOHN
and BERNIE TAUPIN
Slow, but with a beat
mf
Eb
Abmaj7
Bb/D
Gm
1. It's a lit - tle bit fun - ny this feel - ing in - side,
2. If I was a sculp - tor but then a - gain no, or a
4. I sat on the roof and kicked off the moss, well a
5. So ex - cuse me for - get - ting but these things I do,
Cm
Cm/Bb
Cm/A
Ab
I'm not one of those who can eas - i - ly hide,
man who makes po - tions in a trav - el - in' show, I
few of the vers - es, well they've got me quite cross,
You see I've for - got - ten if they're green or they're blue,
Eb/Bb
Bb
G/B
Cm
3
I'm don't have much mon - ey, but, boy, if I did,
know it's not much but it's the best I can do,
But the sun's been quite kind while I wrote this song,
An - y - way the thing is what I real - ly mean,

Eb Fm7 | 1,3 Ab Bb Bbsus Bb

I'd buy a big house where we both could live.
My gift is my song and
It's for peo-ple like you, that keep it turned on.
Yours are the sweet-est eyes

2,4 Ab Eb Ab/Eb Eb Bb/D Cm

this one's for you.
I've ev-er seen.
3. 6. And you can tell ev-'ry-bod-y

Fm7 Ab Bb/D Cm

This is your song. It may be quite sim-ple but,

Fm7 Ab Last time to Coda Cm Cm/Bb

now that it's done, I hope you don't mind, I hope you don't mind

Cm/A Ab6 Eb/G Ab6

that I put down in words. How won - der - ful life is while

rit.

Ab Bb Bbsus Bb **D.S. al Coda**

you're in the world.

a tempo

CODA Cm Cm/Bb Cm/A Ab6

7. 8. I hope you don't mind, I hope you don't mind that I put down in words, How

Eb/G Ab6 | 1 Ab Bb Bbsus Bb

won - der - ful life is while you're in the world.

rit. *a tempo*

2 Ab Eb Ab/Eb Bb/Eb Ab/Eb Eb

you're in the world.

a tempo